ANDY
THE ACTION MAN

Author: Andy Torbet

Boys Power Series 1 of 24

Our Instagram / Facebook page:

Stonefish Publishing

Have you ever dreamed of doing something absolutely incredible? Something full of thrill that not many people would do? For Andy Torbet from Scotland, doing something unexpected is just another day in his life.

If danger, excitement, and mystery are involved, that is exactly where you will find Andy. Not only is he an ex-military man, but he is a stuntman, TV star, explorer, and action man, too!

He began diving at the age of 12 and hasn't never stopped since. He explores magical underwater cave systems and even dives over ancient sunken cities. He dives through reefs that have never been explored before and has discovered new species of marine life.

Andy even finds deep shipwrecks and uncovers the old history that sunk with the ship. Aside from being an underwater adventurer because he is passionate about it, his skills were even used in his time in the military.

Andy spent 10 whole years in the British Forces where he was not only a part of underwater operations like the Army's Underwater Bomb Disposal Team and the Maritime Counter Terrorist Group, but he was a big part of their airborne forces as well.

He was a paratrooper serving with the Airborne Brigade. That is where a trained military soldier is trained to jump from an aircraft using parachutes. However, his time in the sky didn't stop when his time in the military did... no, not at all!

Andy uses a parachute to skydive and a wingsuit to soar through the open skies! He has proven that he is not afraid of speed. Andy once raced a Peregrine Falcon which is the fastest animal in the world!

He has even strapped engines to his legs and reached more than 400kmph in freefall. He is a living, breathing, adventurous stuntman. He has participated in competitions such as the World Speed Skydiving Competition where the top Skydivers can reach speeds up to 600kmph!

If you ever see a man climbing up the side of a flat mountain, there is a chance that it is Andy Torbet. He is a highly experienced rock climber who has discovered new climbing routes in multiple countries, but he didn't stop there!

NNot only is he a rock climber and instructor of rock climbing, but he has also ice climbed from Scotland to Greenland! Incredibly, has climbed icebergs in the Arctic Ocean as well!

He explores caves in the waters, yes, but he explores them on land, too! He has worked in and explored caves all around the world and holds many qualifications as a caver.

Growing up in the Scottish Highlands, Andy's playground wasn't swing sets and slides, it was nature. He spent his early days discovering and exploring. His love for exciting journeys and activities grew, thus creating a true outdoorsman.

Because of his passion for traveling to wild places, he has developed a passion also for the geography, plants, and animals that surround him. So, Andy went on to study further.

Before joining the Forces, Andy began studying zoology, the study of animals, and earned his first degree. And his learning only continued from there! He went on to later earn a degree in Nautical Archaeology, which is learning how humans have interacted with the waters in the past. He sure has gotten use out of that degree through his love of sunken shipwreck discoveries!

He has even worked on his Master's of Archaeology in his "spare time". Aside from stuntman, military man, and explorer, surely an academic can be added to Andy's list of skill sets.

Andy has continued to surprise people with the many things he does, like being a TV Presenter and Filmmaker, too!

Andy has been a presenter on 20 TV series that of course involve action, discovery, or history. He has produced and directed documentary films for clients and film festivals. He has also worked in short films as both an actor and, to no surprise, a stuntman.

When there is a film that involves caving, diving, underwater, or skydiving, Andy often works with the crew to provide his knowledge and special skills to help out.

Not only is Andy Torbet all of those awesome things, he is also an inspiration. He inspires boys all over the world to be daring, to be brave, and to be bold. He teaches others that you don't have to choose just one thing to "be" in life. As long as you are always open to learning and discovering, you can be many great things, all at once.

So, what are you waiting for?

Get out there and explore, discover, and learn!

Safety first, of course.

Printed in Great Britain
by Amazon

18904218R00025